P9-CNG-846

IF YOU WERE A . . .

Ballet Dancer

IF YOU WERE A...
Ballet Dancer

Virginia Schomp

BENCHMARK BOOKS

MARSHALL CAVENDISH
NEW YORK

3 1267 13768 5259

Backstage there may be jitters, but onstage the dancers think of nothing but dancing.

If you were a ballet dancer, you would glide gracefully across a stage. You would leap and twirl in a world of lights, music, and magic.

The next morning, your feet hurt. You get up and practice anyway. Tonight you will dance again, and you want to be perfect.

The curtain rises. You step on stage. You forget your sore feet. You might even forget that hundreds of people are watching. All that would matter is the magic of the dance if you were a ballet dancer.

All ballet dancers—even famous stars—train for hours every day. Dancing is hard work, and training keeps them strong. Practicing the same steps over and over also helps them become even better dancers.

Practice begins with a ballet lesson. Dancers warm up their muscles with exercises. If you took a ballet class, you would warm up at the barre. This long wooden handrail helps you keep your balance as you give each leg a satisfying *strrrrretch*.

Like an athlete preparing for a race, this dancer warms up to prevent injuries in class.

In ballet class, exercises teach gracefulness, balance, and control.

Performing an arabesque, *the dancer stands on one leg, with the other sweeping high behind.*

No dance step is more exciting than ballet's grand jeté.

After warm-up, the dancers practice movements at the barre. They must know how to do hundreds of ballet steps. A teacher calls out the names of the steps in French, the worldwide language of ballet.

Next the dancers move to the center of the floor. Their steps become livelier and more difficult. *"Pirouette,"** the teacher calls, and they whirl around like tops. Small jumps lead to *grand jetés*—exciting leaps through the air.

*For help in pronouncing difficult words, see "Words to Know" on page 31.

The lesson ends and rehearsal begins. The dancers practice the ballets they will be performing. Sometimes the choreographer helps them learn their parts. Choreographers create new ballets by planning the movements to be made by all the performers.

The ballet company's main group of dancers, called the corps de ballet, *work together to learn their parts.*

A special teacher called the ballet mistress helps the star dancers get their steps just right.

The very best dancers have the starring parts in the ballet. A man who is a ballet star is called a *premier danseur*— "first dancer." Top women dancers are called ballerinas. The *prima ballerina* is the company's brightest female star.

Under bright stage lights, faces look pale, so both men and women dancers wear lots of makeup.

By evening, all the dancers have spent hours in class and rehearsals. It's time to get ready for the performance.

If you were a ballet dancer, you would sit at a dressing table. You would put on makeup and style your hair. Now you step into the costume designed for your part in the ballet. Will you wear simple body tights? Or a splendid outfit with ruffles and jewels? Should you pin on a clown's cap or a glittering crown?

White net dresses called tutus add to the beauty of the ballet.

As the dancers get ready, the audience is seated. Beautiful music starts to play. The curtain rises. And in a splash of lights and color, graceful figures fill the stage.

Tonight's performance is *The Nutcracker*. This ballet is about a girl who gets a little wooden nutcracker for Christmas. Her gift comes to life and takes her to a fairyland of palaces and dancing snowflakes.

In The Nutcracker, *costumes, music, and scenery help the dancers tell the story of a magical journey.*

For many ballerinas, nothing is more exciting than dancing the role of the princess in The Sleeping Beauty.

Ballets like *The Nutcracker* tell a story. Some story ballets borrow from old legends and fairy tales. *Cinderella* tells the old tale of a ragged girl who meets her Prince Charming. In *The Sleeping Beauty*, a princess wakes with a kiss from a handsome prince.

Dancers in story ballets are like actors in a play—only these actors tell their story without words. Using movements and expressions, they take the audience to a make-believe world.

Three palace ladies prance off to the ball in Cinderella.

One of the most exciting parts of a ballet is the *pas de deux*—the "dance for two." The steps of the ballerina and *premier danseur* fit together like notes in a song. These dancers have practiced hard to make their movements look easy—even the lifts, when the man sweeps his partner high in the air.

In solos, the stars dance alone. The *premier danseur* shows off stunning leaps and turns. The ballerina's solo is light, graceful, and delicate.

In lifts, the ballerina helps by pushing off the floor at just the right moment.

The Sugar Plum Fairy dances a delicate solo on the tips of her toes in The Nutcracker.

Many modern ballets are a constantly changing picture of light and movement.

Some ballets do not tell a story. Instead they show thoughts or feelings. Like a painting full of odd shapes, modern ballets may try out unusual movements and designs.

If you danced in a modern ballet, you would do more than just perform steps. Like the dancer in a story ballet, you must also play a part. Is your character sad or cheerful? Angry, funny, or *wild*? You would dance those feelings and help the audience feel them, too.

In the powerful ballet Rainbow 'Round My Shoulder, *a prisoner dances his dreams of freedom.*

How do you dance *funny* feelings? You start with a funny story. Then you add lively steps, comical costumes, and lots of smiles.

Even serious ballets may have funny moments. Sometimes these come by accident. Once, during a lift, a ballerina got caught in a fancy ceiling light. The *premier danseur* kept running until he realized his arms were empty. Everyone, including the dancers, laughed as he ran back to grab his partner.

Silly costumes help dancers tell the funny story of The Ugly Duckling.

Cheers from an audience who loved her performance are the ballerina's best reward.

The ballet ends and the curtain closes. If you were a ballet dancer, you would listen as the audience claps and cheers. When the curtain parts again for the "curtain call," you bow to show your thanks.

Will you join your friends for a noisy late-night meal? Or go home to rest your aching feet? Either way, all you can think about is the performance. It's been a long day. But tonight you danced in a magical world, and that has made your hard work worthwhile.

These performers of The Firebird *make their curtain call a show in itself.*

Some children begin taking pre-ballet classes when they are three or four years old.

These young dancers are practicing one of the five basic positions of ballet.

Do you dream of dancing in a beautiful ballet? To make that dream come true, you must start lessons while you are young. By the time you are eleven or twelve years old, you will go to ballet school every day. At seventeen or eighteen, you may join a ballet company.

Imagine whirling with the *corps de ballet*—the company's main group of dancers. Or sharing your love of dance in a *pas de deux*. Someday you might even light up the stage as one of the shining stars of ballet.

Older students spend many hours practicing the basics and learning more difficult steps.

BALLET DANCERS IN TIME

Ballet began 400 years ago in the palaces of French kings and queens.

Soon boys and girls were training to become professional dancers. Ballerinas danced in long heavy skirts and high heels.

Marie Taglioni was the greatest dancer of ballet's Romantic Age. This period in the mid-1800s was a time of magical love stories, with elves, witches, and winged fairies.

Many of the most exciting dancers of the 1900s have come from Russia. Russian ballerina Anna Pavlova's solo in *The Dying Swan* made her famous around the world.

In the 1960s, Rudolf Nureyev and Margot Fonteyn, who had already become superstars dancing on their own, dazzled the world by dancing as partners.

Ballet companies in Europe and the United States borrowed exciting new ideas from the Russians. A French company held this spirited rehearsal in 1937.

A BALLET DANCER'S CLOTHING AND ACCESSORIES

Barre—held for balance

Pointe shoes— special ballet shoes with hardened tips—help the dancer stand on the tips of her toes.

During practice, a leotard and tights let the dancer move easily, and leg warmers keep muscles warm.

In performances of early ballets, women dancers usually wear tutus, while men wear tights and hip-length shirts called tunics.

Makeup—to make faces easier to see from far away

WORDS TO KNOW

barre (bar) The long wooden handrail attached to the walls of a dance studio.

choreographer (kawr-ee-AH-gruh-fer) A person who makes up dances by deciding how the performers will be arranged on stage and what movements they will perform.

corps de ballet (kawr de ba-LAY) The main group of dancers in a ballet company.

grand jeté (grahn zhuh-TAY) A big leap from one leg to the other.

pas de deux (pah de DEU) A dance for two people.

pirouette (peer-uh-WEHT) A way of spinning on one leg.

premier danseur (pruh-meeYAY DAHN-ser) French for "first dancer"; a man who is a leading dancer in a ballet company.

prima (PREE-muh) *ballerina* French for "leading ballerina"; a woman who is a leading dancer in a ballet company.

This book is for Kristyn, gracious, graceful, and strong

Benchmark Books
Marshall Cavendish Corporation
99 White Plains Road
Tarrytown, New York 10591

Copyright© 1998 by Marshall Cavendish Corporation
All rights reserved. No part of this book may be reproduced or utilized in any form or by any means electronic or mechanical including photocopying, recording, or by any information storage and retrieval system, without permission from the copyright holders.

Library of Congress Cataloging-in-Publication Data
Schomp, Virginia, date.
If you were a— ballet dancer / Virginia Schomp.
p.   cm.   Includes index.
Summary: Depicts a typical day for a ballet dancer, from warm-up exercises and lessons,
to rehearsals, preparation, and finally a performance.
ISBN 0-7614-0616-6 (lib. bdg.)
1. Ballet—Juvenile literature. 2. Ballet dancing—Juvenile literature. 3. Ballet dancers—Juvenile literature.
[1. Ballet. 2. Ballet dancing.] I. Title.
GV1787.5.S35 1998   792.8—dc21   97-14154   CIP   AC

Photo research by Debbie Needleman

Front cover: *Stock Boston*, Herb Snitzer

The Stock Market: Paul Barton, 1; Bob Krist, 4 (inset); Mug Shots, 26 (left). *The Image Bank*: Janeart, 2; Grant Faint, 6; CO Rentmeester, 9; Alvis Upitis, 13; Luis Castaneda, 26-27; Lou Jones, 30 (top left); Sobel/Klonsky, 31. *Martha Swope © Time Inc.*: 4-5, 19, 24, 29 (center bottom). *The Picture Cube*: Jean Hangarter, 7; Todd Phillips, 8; Kindra Clineff, 21. *The Image Works*: Larry Kolvoord, 10; Howard Dratch, 11; David Wells, 27 (right). *Jerry Berndt/Boston Ballet*: 12, 30 (bottom right). *Uniphoto Picture Agency*: Bob Llewellyn, 14-15, 30 (top center, top right). *Jack Vartoogian*: 16, 17, 18, 25, 30 (bottom left). *Jack Mitchell*: 20. *Stock Boston*: Bob Daemmrich, 22-23. *Archive Photos*: 28 (top left), 29 (top); Popperfoto, 29 (bottom right). *The Granger Collection, New York*: 28 (top right). *Corbis-Bettmann*: 28 (bottom right). *Mary Evans Picture Library*: 29 (bottom left).

Printed in the United States of America

3 5 7 8 6 4 2

INDEX